Life: Unfastened

Lesley Butterfield

Presentation by *BookLeaf Publishing*

Web: www.bookleafpub.com

E-mail: info@bookleafpub.com

ISBN: 9789357617703

First edition 2022

*For the angels placed in my path, who guided
me, nursed me, fed me, loved me.*

*I am continually grateful to have known this
type of unconditional love, friendship and
support.*

And I used my pen.

Because you told me I could.

ACKNOWLEDGEMENT

To those who said, "You should write more."

Thank you.

The Drive-Thru

It all started with an advertisement for a drive-thru, hot, fresh meal. Free. Courtesy of a local church.

The kids and I were already on that side of town because I drive nearly 40 minutes to take my son, who has autism and learning disabilities, to a therapeutic tutor every day for an hour.

My other three kids and I wait until he finishes his session, and then we all make the 40-minute trek back home, often getting back late in the evening—tired, hungry, and me still having hours of work to do leftover from the day and additional work preparing for tomorrow. This is a snapshot of my life as a single mom.

Before I go on, here are some rhetorical questions that may help put into context my perspectives. In your family and home, who packs the lunches? Who makes sure there is a gallon of unexpired milk in the fridge? Who makes sure the homework folders are stocked with completed homework? Who makes sure every child's mask is clean? Who does flashcards for sight words and times tables? Who hovers in the bathroom to make sure teeth are brushed? Who cleans up dinner? Who makes dinner? Who sets the table? Who does the dishes? Who does bedtime? Who checks for clean undies? Who gets up with children in the middle of the night after a night terror?

Everything I do, as a parent and as a mother, is for my children. This is the MOST important role I have and one that I love and cherish. Working long hours to pay for therapy on my own because my co-parent refuses to contribute is never a second thought for me because my son needs it. Sacrificing hours for my children to be able to have what they need whenever they need it is something I happily do. This goes with also saying that as a single parent, I do not get relief from a husband or partner to pick up slack when I fail at meeting the demands of parenthood (because I do fail—we all fail sometimes.)

When I think of things I am responsible for, it is easy to get overwhelmed. I mean the homework, flashcards, brushing teeth, bathing, packing lunches, packing snacks, signing permission slips, checking homework folders, stocking homework folders, laundry, masks, laundering other clothes, planning dinner, making dinner, cleaning dinner, setting the table, doing the dishes,￼ driving to therapy, paying for therapy, planning enriching activities, signing up for extracurriculars, getting the kids where they need to be at all times AND the list goes on.

Even just having someone to tag team knocking out a few of these things would be helpful each day. But yeah, there is NO ONE but me. To do it all.

And before anyone accuses me of complaining, let me state, yes, I absolutely chose this when considering the alternative of an abusive marriage modeled for my children. Yes, I would choose this again a million times over. Yes, I know this is the typical life of being a single mom.

But here's a big truth bomb: It's hard y'all. Like THE HARDEST thing.
You see, this day was especially tiring. Haircuts for a child who literally feels pain when his hair is being cut, a change in typical routine (also the kiss of death for us autism moms), and balancing online homework (how do you even do this) with regular in-person school.

So between running to therapy, tutoring, haircuts, and back to therapy while coaxing kids to behave and sit down and not look at each other the wrong way, I was just at the wits' end of exhaustion.

So we did it. We went to the advertised "free, fresh, hot meals" drive-thru at a local church.

A kind lady wearing a mask came up a gave me a little mint glued on a notecard with a motivational message about "Encourage-mint." She asked how many meals we needed, and I stated there were five of us. She said, "I'm so glad you came!" like she knew me, and then added, "These meals aren't much but they are warm, and I hope it helps."

Five individual hot spaghetti dinners were brought out to five hungry humans in my minivan. Truthfully, I cannot remember the last time someone made me a hot meal.

This is not a pity party but more an honest, heartfelt acknowledgment of the beautiful mercy that comes from accepting the most needed act of service exactly when it is needed and how powerful this can truly be.

Church workers, wearing matching shirts advertising God, waved me through the drive-thru and smiled as we left.

Shame I did not feel.

Mercy . . . yes. Mercy, love, gratitude. Pure and good and beautiful.

I couldn't even make it out of the parking lot. I pulled into an empty stall—tears suddenly streaming down my face, while the aroma of homemade spaghetti sauce filled the car.

One less thing on my list of unending responsibilities tonight. And it was a little, huge thing. So much that it made me realize . . .

God is in the drive-thru.

The Heaven

Tying the eternal salvation and exaltation of church members to a checklist of requirements, which includes but is not limited to paying money to the church, is spiritual extortion.

Teaching that families may not be together after death because of differences in beliefs, inability to conform, or unwillingness to make specific prescribed covenants is spiritual coercion.

Perpetuating this belief as a universal truth for everyone is psychological torment and religious manipulation.

These teachings are alienating to a myriad of families, including divorced families, blended families, single-parent families, step families, childless families, extended families, grandparent families, foster families, joint families, families by choice, non-nuclear families and LGBTQ families.

It also carelessly promotes "othering" among traditional families because opportunities for learning, growth, connection, empathy and understanding of people in situations that are different but no less worthy, can be stifled by these beliefs.

As a single mother who has had no choice but to step away from the church for my own safety, I see that my children (who still sometimes attend) are damaged and harmed when they hear this rhetoric, as it causes psychological trauma and is emotionally threatening.

No mother should ever have to hear her child ask, "Why can't we be in the same heaven, Mommy?" It is not OK. And it is certainly not healthy.

And as a community health nurse, I find it deeply concerning, ethically speaking, as it is fundamentally indicative of an unhealthy institutional system. The Church of Jesus Christ of Latter-day Saints should not be in the business of spiritual alienation, family separation or ecclesiastical intimidation. But, as it appears, it most definitely is.

Life is not black and white. It is a million shades of gray plus all the colors of the rainbow. Heaven will be just as colorful and vibrant.

I fully embrace the teachings of Jesus Christ, which is why I teach my children that nothing will separate us. Ever. Because this is what Christ taught.

Heaven will be a place of love, not longing.

It will be a place of healing, not hurting.

It will be a place of well-being, not wounding.

It will be a place of peace, not pain.

It will be a place of connection, not coercion.

It will be a place of acceptance, not abandonment.

It will be a place of reception, not rejection.

It will be a place of optimism, not ostracism.

It will be a place of inclusion, not anguish.

It will be a place of tranquility, not trauma.

It will be a place of togetherness, not terror.

It will be a place of safety, not separation.

It will be a place of elation, not encumbrance.

It will be a place of goodness, not grief.

It will be place of happiness, not heartache.

No, time is not running out. We have an eternity
to be with our families, our friends and our
loved ones. And I like this happy heaven better.

The Friend

I was in a toxic, abusive relationship. As I became a victim in my marriage, I felt drawn to a new single sister at church. My husband was controlling, especially of my friendships. He distrusted women with whom I developed close bonds due to shared experiences.

It was as if he feared that my closeness with another would be the pathway to my escape. And eventually, he would be right. This is when I met her. I needed human connection, even though it required whole-hearted vulnerability, something that was difficult for me at the time because of the shame of abuse.

This single sister's story was shockingly similar to mine, which caused me to trust her.

Experiencing the secrecy of abuse, I was desperate for support and connection and it was clear we had these things in common. She had a harrowing story of surviving an abusive marriage herself, a husband who cheated on her with her best friend and spoke of her struggle as a single mom with full custody.

She wore this like a badge of honor. I was taken
by her bravery. At the time, I could never
imagine being in her shoes, having gone through
all she had gone through.

We became intimate friends, walking together in
the mornings, lunching at Panera, bonding over
being a betrayed spouse. Soon, I felt comfortable
enough to confide in her about the abuse I was
experiencing.

I shared my secret with her–I had contacted my
local domestic violence shelter and heeded the
instructions to have a safe place to go and a plan
in place should the time come. Her reply was
empathetic just as I would have expected it to
be.

She also urged me to leave because I "wouldn't
have any trouble finding another guy."

When my children and I fled, I had injuries.
Visible, horrible abrasions and bruising. The
assault gave me flashbacks and nightmares for
weeks.

Soon, I learned that my husband was going to be
asking for custody of the children and was

taking me to court. I had anxiety over what may happen, as my husband held a position of power and respect in our town and I was just a stay at home mom. No one knew of the abuse behind closed doors—no one except my single friend.

Coming back to the place of my abuse was surreal. As I walked into the courthouse, I saw her. My friend who was a single mother, who had a harrowing story of surviving an abusive marriage, whose husband had cheated on her with her best friend, who had full custody of her children.

The friend who wore this like a badge of honor. I was taken by her bravery, thinking "Wow, is she here for me?" Realizing that once a long time ago, I could never imagine being in her shoes and at this moment I was.

But she wouldn't look at or acknowledge me. Nothing could prepare me for what happened next. Soon, I realized that she was there with my husband, for my husband. My abuser.

The shock and horror were earth-shattering.
How could she?

Why?

What?

It soon came none to me that she would proffer
her testimony, stating that I was an unfit mother;
that I planned to kidnap my own children, that
my husband would never abuse me. She bragged
about working as a city employee in social
services and taking children away from unfit
parents.

She took pride in these things; virtue signaling
using the lives of my children as collateral.

I have never felt betrayal like this before.
It flattened my spirit and stamped out so much
of what I thought I knew. It would be years
before I grew to be able to fully trust myself
again after her indescribable actions.

Realization after realization swept over me, that
she was having an affair with my husband, at the
same time my skin was black and blue from his
abuse. She had stayed in my home, carelessly
boxed up my intimate belongings, and
intentionally destroyed my personal possessions.

I see from private chats that they conspired
together from the beginning. Within days of me

fleeing for my life with my children in tow, they were going on hikes together, dating, romancing each other. Realizing she put herself, her career, her livelihood on the line for him–a person she knew was abusive–left me in disbelief day after day after day.

Her betrayal felt as harmful as the physical abuse itself.
Those horrific abrasions and purple bruises faded–her damage still lingers.

People who hear my story for the first time will often say: "She did what!?" Truthfully, I can never forgive her (and she has not asked) for betraying me in a way that only a woman would understand—using my children in her plan, hurting me in such a fundamental and cheap way; by attacking my mothering.

Because it was the most important role I held.

But still- I have overcome this. I have risen from the ashes to become an advocate, a writer, a nurse who helps others survive and thrive in spite of trauma.

But I am still, always, and most importantly a mother.

The Tomatoes

Do you know what it is like to not trust yourself? Everything is upside down and backwards and all you can do is float through your own life like a helpless spectator who forgot to take off her cheap 3-D glasses when the movie was over. If you do, you may have a past like mine. I was the wife of a serial adulterer.

Looking back, I try to decipher every situation of my former life. It feels as if I'm decoding some ancient, foreign language without the translation key. So many emotions. So many. I suffered in silence all those years because I knew it must be my fault he was going to other women. Something was wrong with me. What else would be the issue?

Certainly, it couldn't be him. This idea was reinforced by many people in my life. My bishop told me I would have the greater sin by divorcing my husband, my family expressed concern about eternal bonds I would be breaking, my friends shared that they had experienced adultery and come through it with better, stronger marriages. It was all on me, not him. Some intentionally reinforced that he wasn't the problem, others unintentionally. But they reinforced, nonetheless.

It must be me.

That was my very real scripting when I was living the life as a wife of a serial adulterer. And it nearly broke me.

One particular discovery day (which I have come to refer to as D-Day) happened when I was 34 weeks pregnant with my fourth child. We didn't have money to pay for beautiful maternity photos, so I convinced him to take photos of me at home. Of course, my huge and growing belly was the source of self-consciousness but I trusted him and believed he loved me no matter how deep my stretch marks grew. Later that day, my smile faded and my joy turned to bewilderment with the revelation that our marriage, our baby, all our children were compromised by the selfish, irresponsible and unbelievable actions of the person I loved and trusted.

Awful, awful, awful day. So incredibly awful. From that point, there would be multiple D-Days as regular as bombs going off in the middle of a world war. Years worth of more revelations and more affairs. More meaningless indiscretions. On one particular day, I found out about three of the other women. How did I react? I went to Walgreens and spent $200 on wrinkle cream and diet pills.

Fix myself, be more desirable, become skinnier, look younger. Juggling thoughts of worthlessness while caring for four young children under the age of 5, I lived everyday in a minefield. And of course, I smiled like a Christmas card family, pretended everything was perfect. Because the real shame of infidelity falls on the woman who is the victim of it. She must be a prude, she must not be doing her duty as a wife, she must be cold, unfeeling.

It must be me.

Betrayal trauma is especially damaging because of who it is committed by and against whom it is committed. As a wife, I trusted my husband. People don't get married thinking they can't trust their spouse. Just the opposite: people likely trust their spouse with their lives. (For time and all eternity!)

You trust them to love you despite all the reasons they could find they shouldn't–the weird dimples on your butt, your skin with visible flaws when the makeup is washed away, your tenuous family issues that fester from childhood wounds, the fact that you managed to burn Kraft Macaroni and Cheese. The deep-down insecurities that no one else knows about except the person sleeping next to you every night. And then that person–the person who knows you so intimately, the person who you completely trust–betrays that trust in ways that are unimaginable… The subtle gaslighting, the thoughtless comments, the cleverly disguised degradation, the lies and manipulation that permeate all aspects of your life together. It is far more damaging than a stranger's betrayal. It is personal, intimate treason.

It must be me.

I think a lot of the processing also comes with the fact that over and over again, I would convince myself that I was safe. That he was in therapy. That he promised to never do it again. That he saw how much it hurt and devastated me. That of course he would fix this to keep our family intact.

When in reality: I wasn't safe. Therapy became another way to justify his unvirtuous actions. Promises were broken. He saw the hurt but didn't care. He chose instant gratification over our beautiful family. Time and time again. I have learned, by experience, that the myth of a woman scorned is merely a negative, stereotypical blame-shifting trope. A scorned woman is likely one that has experienced life-altering trauma. Don't reduce that to thinking her ego was bruised. Her soul, her life, her reality was smashed to bits and then some.

It must be me.

I can still remember the teeny tiny bits of the hope that I would feel when I would think, This time, this time it will work. This is the time he will get control of this. This is the time he will stop this harm and hurt. This is the time that we can truly heal. This hope felt so good. A big stream of fresh water in the middle of a scorched-earth desert. But my hopes would inevitably be dashed with more revelations of infidelity.

Soon, I learned that my hope could not be dependent on his actions. I am not sure what exactly led me to that life-saving realization, other than a few very loving and trusted souls. Two of them were my visiting teachers, assigned to visit me by the same Church that had been browbeating me into staying in the marriage. These women, pure and good women, lit the way; they led the way for me to leave.

Hope started to build and resilience formed, little by little, once I stopped looking to him to provide approval and assurance. I could cultivate it on my own. It was the difference between canned vegetables served on a cafeteria tray and picking a perfect vine-ripened tomato grown from a tiny little seed in your own garden.

It must be me. Suddenly that painful mantra evolved, became new and empowering. It must be me—it is me. It has always been within me.

Me, who could love myself. Me, who could grow my own perfect tomatoes.

Healing trauma like this is so painful. Some days, it comes from nowhere and sits on my shoulders, a literal burden that I carry. Other days it is a heavy cloud of thick grief for the naïveté that I lost. There really is not much band-aid healing, just learning to live with scar tissue.

I had it within me. The entire time: the fight, the hope, the healing, the drive, the determination, the little tomato seed.

It must be me.

The Letter

I received the news on this white snowy day that my sealing was cancelled. The letter came in an official envelope marked from the Office of the First Presidency.

This means the spiritual, covenanted marriage between my former spouse and I is finally undone. Erased in the imaginary book of heaven.

My tires spun, stuck in the snow as I was grabbing the letter out of the mailbox. How strange to know this final symbolic tie is severed then only to be stuck in the sticky sludge. With my really old mom van, a vintage motif to my Mormon roots.

I thought I would feel celebratory. But it felt tiring. And almost—worthless. My tires spun. And stuck. And spun.

After months of asking, writing, petitioning, researching, waiting, meetings, and lots of follow-ups, it was finally done. Was it worth the trauma if it all? Putting myself through having to write out all the betrayals and pain again—in order to justify the permission to cancel this ordinance to those that claim only they have the power to do it.

I don't know. I don't know if I will ever know.

I feel—free. But I've felt free, already.

I feel—peace. But I've felt peace, already.

I feel—content. But I've felt content, already.

So I sat—watching the sun go down over the blanket of a field of white, sitting amidst boxes packed of my home that I thought would be forever, holding this letter on official stationary, listening to the silence of fresh starts, it all felt—strangely beautiful.

The snow was dripping off icicles that had formed, as the sun grew dark, and grey clouds set in. It was cold and will soon be icy and black. But I knew tomorrow the warm sun will show and the field of white will lay undisturbed until it fades to green, a new home will soon be created, and the letter will still be just a letter.

I didn't need the letter.
I didn't need the home.

I didn't need the validation of someone telling
me that what happened was awful.
I didn't need to say say say it again for them.
They knew. Already.

I needed the beauty of knowing the sun will
come.
The snow will melt.
The tires will unstick.
The home will be loved.
The soul will move forward.
The joy will grow greater.

And
The letter is just a letter.

The Fairy Tale

As little girls in the church, we are taught the fairy tale: find a boy that meets the checklist, marry a returned missionary—in the temple of course, have lots of babies, don't think too much about important things like a career, because you'll have a happy life either way, and yay--you get your eternity. This is also called the Plan of Salvation.

After my transition away of the church and divorce (simultaneously), I began to see how the fairy tale I was told and sold was so incredibly false. False AND damaging. To women AND men. SO wrong in so many ways--its sets couples up for unrealistic expectations, places emphasis on the transactional nature of relationships rather than it focusing on being mutually fulfilling and offering meaningful connection for both parties. We tend to think of marriage as a trade-off: men provide financially and bring the priesthood to the home, while women give babies, become domesticated, often giving up talents, hopes, and their life dreams as a benevolent sacrifice for the family. This fairy tale paints a rosy gloss over real challenges that families face. It also does not place much emphasis on finding real, true, deep, intimate connection, but instead--just a surface level fairy tale scenario where two people who meet each others checklists can get married for eternity and viola--they are on their way to the celestial kingdom. READ: Meh—you'll figure it out, and don't worry much if you don't, because you get eternal salvation in the end, and that should be worth anything you are giving up to have it.

This fairy tale has roots in exceptionalism, which Mormonism also is planted. Exceptionalism is how we as a (religious) culture justify being "blessed" with the word of God, when no one else has is. It is how we who have "eternal marriages" or "eternal families"would justify that blessing--when most of the world does not have the opportunity. We are chosen, we are the exception. We have to believe in Exceptionalism as Mormons because if we don't, the world would not make sense.

I've met a lot of people while dating. Recently, one particular person reflected to me my value without realizing it. This someone dropped everything to help me move my entire house in a weekend and then came back the next day and unpacked my whole kitchen and organized my canned goods. He hung up all my clothes and wasn't weird about me having 50 pairs of shoes or boxes of expired mac and cheese. He just was there. Like really present. He also didn't ask anything of me.

When I got triggered moving from my gorgeous home that where I raised my kids, that I thought would be a forever home, he didn't get upset or act weird. He was patient and kind. And understanding. No, he did not label me as dramatic or crazy or too high-maintenance. He shared parts of his life where he felt similar feelings. This is empathy and it is beautiful and rare.

Then, me being who I am, start analyzing this great great great thing and wonder:
"What on earth does he want from me?"
"Why is he being so nice?"
"He must want ________."
"He wouldn't do service just because, so why is he doing this?"
"What's in it for him?"

And I start convincing myself that I am not worthy of being loved just for me because I do not believe in exceptionalism anymore. Because this is a Mormon thing that I reject. I'm not exceptional and I'm not an exception, I do not believe in the fairy tale. I am not giving him anything, so why is he serving me, without wanting anything in return and what is he getting out of this? There is literally nothing in it for him.

It never occurred to me that he just wanted to spend time with me—that was all and that was enough. It didn't matter if we were packing pots and pans and wearing sweats. I didn't need to look perfect, be perfect, or offer him anything in return. I didn't need to sacrifice my dreams to prove I was worthy. I didn't need to make him dinner or even pretend like I am a decent cook. I didn't need to have all the boxes labeled with "ITEMS CONTAINED WITHIN" like a good Mormon girl would have. It didn't need to be a dream date with roses or a fancy dinner. It was actually muddy and cold and we hauled heavy shit up and down staircases. And that was enough. It was all just enough.

But I could not get over why why why?

This is what I grieve---the simple ability to accept love, friendship, true service, true giving, and even sincere interest from another person because of my experiences that have told me and

showed me that I am an object to provide ______
for someone else and I do not have worth unless
I am providing _____ for someone else.

The thought that someone would just like me for
me and expect nothing in return feels like a
foreign language that I do not speak. I feel like
an infant learning to crawl.

But learning to crawl is a fun and beautiful
thing. Yes, there will be bumps and bruises and
red knees. I will need enough sturdy furniture to
grab onto for when I fall—it is sure to hurt. But I
will get back up and keep trying. Keep learning.
Keep growing.

And one day, I will run fast and strong and I will
know my value is inherently in me.

Like it was all along.

The Wounds

Preschool, Scholar of the Year. The yellow laminated star pinned, paper crown placed. Running home, would someone to tell me, "Now you are loved. Now you are good. Now you are enough."

Grade school, reports cards lined capital S's for Satisfactory. "A joy to have in class." "Truly a model student," written in cursive. Holding tight, riding home, hoping someone would tell me, "Now you are loved. Now you are good. Now you are enough."

Middle school, straight A student. Extra credit everything. Struggling inside. Needed someone to say to me, "Now you are loved. Now you are good. Now you are enough."

High school, top ten percent. National Honor Society. Still waiting for someone to tell me, "Now you are loved. Now you are good. Now you are enough."

College, class valedictorian. Lots of congratulations, but not from the ones that mattered. Could they just say, "Now you are

loved. Now you are good. Now you are
enough.”

Married young. To someone who also couldn’t
and wouldn’t say, “Now you are loved. Now you
are good. Now you are enough.”

Did all the things they told me to. Gave up a life
for another’s. Mine was not as important. Was
never told “Now you are loved. Now you are
good. Now you are enough.”

Did the hardest thing ever. Became a single
mom. Gave up listening for “Now you are loved.
Now you are good. Now you are enough.”

Hurt by a system that should have helped. And
validating my pain means questioning what they
know. So they can’t say, “Now you are loved.
Now you are good. Now you are enough.”

My little girl drew me a picture. Colored on torn
piece notebook paper. Edges frayed. Imperfect,
hurried. She only had one crayon—ugly, green,
dull. Her face beaming—looking for validation
she already knows I will give her.

“You are loved. You are good. You are always
enough.”

The Meadow

The last few years have been rough. I had lost a large part of my community at the same time I was losing a family and a life that I dreamed of. It was like those things—were there one minute and evaporated the next. A lot of trauma and living in a constant state of survival mode and pivoting to the next fire. (Many of you know this.) And not long ago, I had a physical manifestation of that stress that landed me in the hospital hooked up to an overpriced IV, because my body simply shut down and said "no more." (Many of you do not know this.)

What I have learned—is that things burning to the ground can be so beautiful. Yes, full of heartache. Sadness. Grief. But renewal, perspective and so much growth can be gained in this process. And this is something I would never ever trade for the world.

It has taken a long time for me to get to a place where my heart did not hurt most of the time. Where I my eyes would no longer well up with tears when I would think about the things that have happened. Where I didn't like I was

carrying a heavy load of palpable grief with me
everywhere.

I recently started to explore and be intentional
about guided meditation, breathwork, energy
healing and Havening. I've had so many
breakthroughs, most are intensely private and
sacred to me. But one in particular that I can
share:

I was walking along on a path in the wilderness.
I suddenly came up on thick dark woods but I
could see light peaking through them. I walked
through the dark woods, hearing the twigs snap
under my feet and feeling the cool mist of the
forest around me. When I reached the edge, the
forest opened to a gorgeous expansive field with
wildflowers and tall prairie grass that rippled
like waves in the breeze. There were majestic
mountains in the distance, also so beautiful. But,
I did not want to keep going. Instead I wanted to
rest there, in the wildflower field, on an old
quilted blanket, wearing a flowy cotton summer
dress staring up at the sky and watching the
clouds roll by.

"Do you want to keep going?" again the
question asked.

"No" my subconscious answered.

This wildflower field is where I want to be for now. Then, the thought came,

"This is where I want to build my home."

Yes, the mountains were gorgeous and sure, I'd like to hike them one day, but not now. That can wait. I just got done stumbling through these thick dark woods behind me. I want to just build my home on this piece of earth, stable and calm, so I can rest here and enjoy these wildflowers. I do not need to seek, explore, or conquer those mountains in the distance now. I can be content right here, right now, in my wildflower field.

In healing, reflection, and learning, and guidance, I have found the most beautiful souls. People who have guided me to see that I don't have to hang on to hurt and pain. People who have helped me turn my healing inward and make it private when it needed to be. People who have helped me to step back and look at situations from other perspectives that I failed to see. People who have taught me how to love with vulnerability and how to say goodbye with honesty. People who have given me permission to focus on giving to myself—as much as I give to others. And to let go of the things that are no longer serving me. People who have led me to find my wildflower field, shown me how to pick the flowers that grow there. Plant others that I want to grow there. And enjoy them all.

I have truly experienced so much growth and progress while sitting in my wildflower field—which is strange because I thought all I was doing was resting here a while. Friendships gained, relationships nurtured, opportunities for growth, loving goodbyes manifested, chances to choose forgiveness, and weights of grief and hurt in mind and body lifted while so much confidence and peace was gained. I feel healthy, beautiful, and vibrant inside and out.

And now, I can rest. I can wait. I can enjoy. Partake. Learn. Grow. Love. Live. However I want and however that looks—it will be beautiful. Because it is my field. My home. And my wildflowers.

The Rehab

I bought a fixer upper. Out of fear mostly. I was SO scared I was going to get thrown out on my ass during my divorce that I scraped together enough to get a small house with a crappy loan, but it was mine. Mine.

Inside, it was sad-looking, dark, closed off. A perfect metaphor for my own self at certain times over these past few years. Though, as we survive, we also rise and when I rise I tend to see beauty, feel hope, and live joy. And beauty, hope, and joy are what my only goals would be when I embarked on lovingly rehabing this home.

It has been a labor of love over the past year. It has brought healing, focus, and purpose to me when sometimes life has been overwhelming and hard. On late nights alone I have painted and nailed, listening to Trevor Hall sing about his bowl of light and, of course, the occasional true crime podcast. I have come across some interesting parallels while working on this house—gutting it entirely—and rebuilding it from the inside.

-I have been intentional in taking the time to
pick out every fixture, each paint swatch, and let
my imagination lead the way and tell me what it
wants for this home. Everything contained
within this house brings me joy, which reminds
me a of beautiful mantra that I came across in
my meditations that whispered: I get to decide
what to place within my spiritual container. I
want it to carry the most beautiful things. And it
does.

-There is such power in make ugly things
beautiful and purposeful and comforting. It
occurred to me that this home—so cozy,
feminine, perfectly cute— is the dollhouse I did
not have—because I wouldn't let myself
entertain the thought of make-believe because of
its impracticality. Impractical things used to
serve no purpose for my for logical brain, until I
began to see that they do. They lend themselves
to opening our imagination to hope—and this is
the lifeblood of resilience.

-When I purchased this home, it was sad looking
(see before pics in post) . It had dated wood
paneling and horrible carpet, the stairs were one
step away from caving in, and old linoleum floor
was peeling up in various places. So many

people overlooked the home, others laughed when I talked about my vision for it. I saw it though. I saw the potential for it to be beautifully fantastically gorgeous. This is true for anything. Anything has potential for beauty—if you look past the surface.

-There is no greater feeling than finishing something that has taken a really long time to complete. I sometimes wonder if this is what we feel when we get older and near the end of life. Regardless—I want to live in such a way that this is how I want to feel at the end of mine.

-Giving to yourself is never a "gift"—it is a necessity. You deserve to have beautiful surroundings that bring joy. That remind you of beautiful places, people, things. I wanted a weightless hammock swing in my living room, to cradle me in the sunlight the streams through the patio window in the afternoons, so I did it—without a thought of anything else. Nothing else matter except your opinion. You are your own priority. Make any and all of your decisions with that in mind.

The Choice

I was several weeks pregnant with my seventh pregnancy. I had three beautiful children, but also suffered 3 miscarriages during the span of six years.

It was my 4th miscarriage. And it was heartbreaking—because yes, I wanted this baby desperately. We wanted this baby for our family. But perhaps the most devastating aspect about it was the fact that I was carrying a nearly 10 week old fetus that had not yet died inside of me. It would die—there was no doubt about that—you see the heartbeat was 70bpm, far to low from the normal 160bpm to be viable.

Having suffered 3 prior miscarriages and being traumatized by each one—I'll spare the details but suffice it to say that no one should ever go to the bathroom with cramps and suddenly pass a small embryo. I could hold them in my palm. What I could not do was grieve them because I was simply too shocked. I grieve now for the inability I had to grieve then. It should have been different. It likely could have been different.

So my choices with this 4th (soon to be) miscarriage were to wait for the impending death of this embryo or take what is known as the abortion pill. I struggled with this decision greatly. I locked myself in a room—the room that was to be the nursery for this baby. I painted the entire room, while listening to church songs about faith and hope. I was pro-life at this time in my life. I grew up Christian, conservative. Never could I imagine intentionally causing the end of a life growing inside of me. I cried out, I yelled at god, I sobbed so hard. Was it dead yet? Was it slowly dying? What if my body didn't expel it and I have to go back to the ultrasound room? I couldn't go back there again. What if it took weeks? Would I start cramping suddenly in the grocery story picking up a gallon of milk for the family? What if I start to pass it in the car line at school? What if I couldn't handle the pain this time? What would I do? Where would I go? Who would help with my other kids? I was plagued by thoughts of worry and anxiety over the situation. Not because I didn't know what to expect, but because I did.

I had everyone telling me what I should do. People close to me had their own opinions about how I *should* handle MY experience—this private sacred experience of grieving this loss in all its complexities in the way that was best for me. How could they even ever say how I *should* do this? Did they pass these embryos alone on the bathroom floor? Did they hold them in the palm of their hand? Did they wonder if it was breaking a law to flush it down the toilet? There is no handbook on what to do when an embryo falls out of you. Did they weep for their inability to grieve these losses? Did they have nightmares where they could feel the pain all over again?

No. They didn't.

I did.

I came to my answer in a moment of peace—after a particularly sobbed-filled fit of heartache: It was ok. I was ok. My choice was my choice, and I was ok in making the choice that was the best for me.

God.Did.Not.Care.What.Choice.I.Made.

Peacefully, I could clear my schedule. Peacefully, I could make sure my other children were taken care of. Peacefully, I could lay in my bed and cry all weekend and—peacefully, I

could know the approximate day I would pass
and be able say goodbye to this one.

Peacefully.
And privately.
The way it should be.

I changed my views on abortion after this. I
knew that pro-choice was essential to the health
of women, because having this choice was
essential to my well-being. Sadly, I could not see
what women experience in these difficult
situations until I experienced it for myself. That
likely shows I have a lot to learn. I am ashamed
to have been so judgemental of women who
have had to make choices no one ever wants to
make before I had to also make this choice.

But the point of this all is—we have a choice.
Peacefully.
And privately.
The way it should be.

The Mother's Days

I'd like to give a glimpse of what Mothers Day may look like for a single mother.

Scrolling through my feed, I see moms surprised with breakfast in bed, beautiful flower arrangements, brunch out at a fancy restaurant. This looks so nice, I think. The next thought is, but that's not my life.

And before I let any self-pity form, (I know better than to live there) I think of the ways single mothers continually rise to the challenge. We don't have time or energy to spend giving to pity ourselves. There is work to do and no one else to do it but us. There are roles to fulfill and we are literally one person filling all of them. Each day, I wear at least 20 different hats from my single-mom-supply-closet to give my children all they need and deserve.

Mother's Day is Laundry. Folding. Mopping. Lunches. What appointments are this week and how am I going to navigate them with work? Homework. Study guides. Spend time connecting. Help this child with that situation.

Call and arrange ____. Coordinate the calendar.
Figure out ways to make it all work. And it
usually does alway work.

Somehow.

(Because we do it.) We do it so hard that it's
second nature by now. Silly pancakes in bed and
expensive brunch out— what would I even do
with a huge bouquet of flowers anyway? Sounds
exhausting to just get all the kids ready in some
nice clothes, to be frank. I'd have to dig in some
closet somewhere to find a button up shirt that
doesn't have Spider-Man graphics on it. And
don't get me started on dress shoes. Because
yeah— ain't none of those around here. And,
that's ok.

Single moms usually never plan for their life to
turn out this way. But it is this way and here we
are. And while I still love my life, yes— it looks
different than I thought it would. Than I
dreamed it would.

Pancakes and flowers and brunch— yes you
caught me— sure, I wish I had those things
today.

But—

What a gift it is that I could learn so much about myself, step into my own authority, build my confidence as a woman, and learn the special abilities I have to do all the things.

What a gift it is when I hear no less than 20 times a day, "Mom, where is my ___? Mom, can you do ____ for me? Mom—I need help. And, Mom—I love you."

What a gift it is that we've created a home where we practice grace and love and forgiveness and belonging because these are things we always need.

What a gift it is that they have memories of gluing crap on old sweaters to make ugly Christmas sweaters for school (because there's no way I'm going to actually buy one), then as adults realize that these things were made special and fun because they were loved and what mattered to them mattered to me.

What a gift it is for them to remember how we would hunt for trinkets and treasures at Goodwill, once because we had to, but later because we want to.

What a gift it is for them to remember the
impromptu birthday parties, thrown for each one
of them during the Covid with stuffed animals as
guests and homemade scavenger hunts for party
games, because they were loved and they
deserved their day to be special regardless of
something like a pandemic.

What a gift it is for them to grow up and
remember how nearly every single day mom
would spend her evenings shuffling them to
important therapies, appointments, and how we
do it despite being tired from the day and
sometimes exhausted, because there was no
other option. And it was all for them.

What a gift it is that my kids can see me take
time for myself whenever I need it—its not just
on a special occasion that I "get" to do that. It's
a regular occurrence for me to show them how
to protect my own energy and engage in self
care—for my own survival and for theirs too.

THE SOLs

The SOLs. Standards of Learning, also known as the literal NIGHTMARE of any parent to a child who is differently abled.

But, with the help of a lot of dedication and a specialized tutoring program, called, Fit Learning, my beautiful, capable,intelligent, autistic son, who also has diagnosed learning disabilities, passed his middle school Math and Reading SOLs. FOR THE FIRST TIME EVER.

And not only did he pass—he blew them away!

I am one proud mom. We work SO hard—every single day going to this unique therapeutic tutoring program—and it is worth every bit of time invested and every penny spent. We study differently, we learn what works and we reject things that don't. Even if they are the "gold standard." Because usually that means they are the gold standard for neurotypical students. Neurodiverse individuals are left out of the equation completely.

Kids can do AMAZING things when you give them to tools that let them learn in the way they can. I can't tell you how many times I was told that he may never pass and I needed to start thinking of alternative tracks.

Disability does not mean inability.

Say that out loud.

Disability does not mean inability.

The sooner our systems and our society start to reframe outdated assumptions, the sooner we can all start to grow more together and learn more from each other.

The Covid

Years ago, I left it all. My home, my marriage, my community. I left it all because I had not choice. It was myself and my four kids. I found myself, as a single mom, having to navigate finding housing, obtaining food stamps, getting on Medicaid, weeding through social services and supports. Filling out papers, while bottle feeding my youngest who was still in diapers. Oh the diapers—I sold my plasma to buy those. And the WIC office?—that was like preparing to go into battle, taking four young kids into appointments each month that sometimes took hours.

But through all this, I learned that I could advocate for myself and my children. That I had resilience in me that was unmatched. That I was resourceful. That I could do hard things.

Several years later, I was glued to the tv. News reports that Covid-19 had made its way to US soil was broadcast on stop. The map of America soon lit up like a Christmas tree, red spots everywhere—no places untouched. But this was no gift of course. It was terrifying, traumatizing, and tremendously stressful.

At work, we had conference calls to debrief, we shared fears of running out of supplies, feelings of isolation, and everyone expressing shock about being so alone with just their kids and having a question mark looming over the future like a heavy black rain cloud. My children and I hunkered down in our home too—and I remember feeling as though I had been here before. Because, well, I had.

My thoughts turned to that time not long ago, where I was alone, with my children, trying to find the light under the darkness of that big looming question mark of uncertainty that hung over life like a thick thunderstorm waiting to burst. I had been fearful of scarcity because I experienced scarcity. I had familiar feelings of isolation because I have felt isolated. I had experienced that darkness many times before.

But—the difference was that I knew the ending! I knew what would happen after the rain poured—it would stop! And eventually the sun would rise again. Glorious new growth would pop up in those once dark places, hope would renew even stronger and life would find a way to go on as it always does.

I realized that this was a gift. It was the beautiful gift of being a single mother. I knew the strength of myself already. I knew the outcome of the situation as scary as it may be—I would land on my feet like I had many times before. I would provide for my children no matter the circumstances because I have always figured out a way to do this for them.

When society was busy buying up endless rolls of toilet paper, and calling out the calvary of babysitters, I'll bet the single moms were calmly, quietly whispering to their babies, "Do not worry, my child—I've always got you. No matter the obstacle we will get through it. We always do."

You see, Covid was simply just one obstacle of many in the life of those who live day to day in the crux of making ends meet. For those who have lived in survival—surviving is just a daily thing we do. It is nothing new—running out of toilet paper or wondering who will watch our kids when we have to go to work. We make it work a thousand different ways a thousand different days.

I shared these thoughts on a debriefing conference call one afternoon with some of my trusted coworkers. I showed them a garden I planted with my kids over the weekend and the set up we had implemented for homeschool, complete with various stations, a handwritten schedule, and a list of resources I compiled late one night while scrolling though Facebook. I showed them how I gave my daughter a makeshift birthday party the day before with her stuffed animals as her guests and a cake we made from the pantry. They had a million questions and a million compliments. In that moment, I felt pride as a single mom—something that I assure you is not typical.

Society tends to view us a drain on resources or even a detriment to the system, we are placed last so often. But if you take time to look closely, listen intently and learn just a little, you may just see that we have valuable perspectives to offer to any situation.

I think back on this time with a great fondness now. Yes, it was stressful. Yes I felt alone. Yes, we were isolated. But the connectedness and grounding that my children and I felt while together was so special.

Perhaps the biggest and best gift is the fact that my children were there to see and witness and take it all in the entire time. I can only hope that the impression of seeing their mother do it on her own for them, over and over again, will enhance their own beliefs in the tremendous value of women, mothers, and families who may look different from the norm.

Tonight, while tucking my daughter in bed, she shows me her all her "kids" (which are random stuffed animals tucked in tightly under the covers). She is beaming with pride and joy, as she kisses them each goodnight, just like I do with her.

And I realize, I don't have to hope for these impressions to be made—they already are.

The Men

I want to share something that I have learned and experienced recently, having to do with relationships—namely the romantic kind.

Since my divorce, I have started dating here and there. What started out as a self-effacing joke (joining a dating app in my 40s was my literal definition of a nightmare), turned into being a beautiful process of personal growth in so many ways.

Having experienced a history of systemic trauma caused and perpetuated mostly by men in a high-demand religious community and also in previous relationships—-I was so pessimistic about the opposite sex. It was hard for me to trust men. It was nearly impossible for me to let a man serve me or treat me without getting in my head too much about the expectations that came along with it. Mostly I felt like men would never understand or appreciate me for me. The real me.

I have engaged in so much personal healing work over the past few years as well. Learning to trust myself most of all was one hurdle that I struggled with greatly. This came from frequently being conditioned to outsource my own authority to others (mostly men) who claimed they knew what was best for me, told me what I should want, even claimed to have the power to be the conduit in my own relationship with God.

As I have untangled much of this ball of yarn—so tightly wound up in knots within itself—I have learned and claimed and stepped into my own authority to decide what is best for me. What I want in life. What I need in a relationship. I am own conduit for anything that involves me. No one else.

This is a beautiful, peaceful, powerful realization to claim.

What happens next is sort of a domino effect—after stepping into my own authority, showing up authentically as me, and doing this work to know exactly what I want and and need—the universe seems to whisper— 'There you are my child, finally we can get to work.'

The quality of men that have been placed in my path has been simply amazing. Lovely, lovely beautiful humans. Men who claim their divinely masculine qualities—confident, disciplined, self-controlled, action-taking, logical, boundaried men.

Men who want to have conversations about Viktor Frankel, existentialism, fixed vs. growth-mindset, meditation and even share about the healing work they have done. Men who ask me about the latest book I'm reading. Men who aim for stimulating interactions all the time—every time. Men who want to tell me about their feelings and freely express them. Men who accept responsibility for their stuff. Men who are good and honest and true. Men who are CEOs, tri-athletes, entrepreneurs, public speakers, goal-oriented, pensive, insightful, successful, and know what they want in life. Men who have qualities that match mine. Thank you, universe. I've met so many inspiring and lovely men that I have thoroughly enjoyed getting to know. I while I keep my love life mostly private, but trust me when I say there is a lot of love about this process.

Perhaps of the most surprising things for me to learn is that there are men who like me for my mind and my intellect more than for my body. This was also a big realization to come to.

Having received a lot of messaging in the culture I was raised, specifically where much emphasis was placed on what a woman can provide by means of her body—physical pleasure for a man, bearing children for him, domestic labor for him, caretaking of him—this was a difficult thing to extricate from my sense of self. And even from my life purpose.

Again, as I messily unpacked and untangled the suitcase of knots of balled up yarn—slowly but surely the strings began to unravel into raw material that could be made into any beautiful piece of art I desired. My heart began to open to the realization that I have so much to share and give. I show up as myself—strong, powerful, thoughtful, determined, ambitious, intellectual—every single time, wearing my coat of many colors. What I want is waiting for me and it exists.

This is such a change from the previous silencing and muting of myself and my traits to fit into someone else's definition of what they want in a woman. Dulling my colors so someone else could more comfortable is a thing of the past. My person would love my colors and have his own that shine just a brilliant.

This beautiful truth allows me to have a much more positive, authentic, and real dating experience. It also allows me to say a loving goodbye when it is clear that something is not the right connection for me. There is no trying to stuff all my energy, wants, hope, desires, love, and qualities into someone else's container that is just too small to hold space for all my parts. The container for me will be expansive enough for all my parts and have room for me to grow too. And it's out there!

When we do the work on ourselves—
Our life changes in ways we never imagine. I now feel so hopeful and optimistic that quality men exist and I really appreciate that they have been placed in my path. It is always the right time to decide how you will show up, who you spend your valuable time with, what you will and will not accept, and what is ultimately most important to you. Raise the bar for you because you can. They will rise to meet it—I assure you.

Thank you men—for doing your work and showing me that you can be equal partners, communicate in healthy ways, and that you can place value on connecting on many levels with a woman in order to have a quality relationship.

Finally it occurs to me that just as men played a part in so much of my trauma—they have also been, to a certain extent, an important step in my healing from it.

And that is another beautiful, peaceful, powerful realization.

The Forgiveness

I've recently embarked on the work of forgiveness—because it felt right for me to explore this concept at this time in my journey.

I have learned and experienced so many beautiful things in this bumpy ride trying to marrying myself to the idea of for-give-ness. Sometimes it feels like a reluctant groom, jilting me at the altar, other times he hand delivers grand bouquets of roses and baby's breath. "Forgiveness is for giving," as Trevor Hall says in one of my favorite songs. The root word of forgiveness is the Latin word "perdonare," meaning to give completely.

I was stuck on this part for a while, a long while. If I was honest with myself—I already gave. I didn't like that now I was expected to give some more. Like enough already. More free, gifted (read: expected) undervalued labor that I didn't feel like I wanted to give. I had already given everything I had. I had given all of me all the time. I completely gave completely. I was so tired of giving. I gave my promises, my time, my hopes, my womb, my body, my career, my choices, my individuality, my years of life, my options, my dreams, my every last little and big thing. I gave me. And I gave me.

And I gave me.

Until I had no me left to give.

And some will say, this is what good women do. And others will say, that is your own fault. And there are those who will say, you were foolish to give to freely. But those who understand, they say nothing because they know.

And I know too.

Recently, while doing somatic release work (which I highly recommend after traditional therapeutic processing)—-it hit me like a wave that I could not hold back. A tsunami in my body of a very particular emotion was accessed so easily—but see this feeling was not recent. It was an old pain, from a situation that was not harming me anymore and hasn't for a long time. It was healed ten times over. It was poked and prodded and examined and mulled over in therapy until it stood so objective in my psyche. I could talk about this feeling and the attached circumstances without any emotion whatsoever,

an indication to my objectivity of my healing.
(Or so I thought.)

So it quiet literally shocked me when this
emotion flooded my body with just a few
somatic movements. It was a rough,
heart-wrenching, familiar, accessible,
freely-flowing and fresh feeling that I had not
felt in many years. It hurt deep in my heartspace.
A wound whose ache was still there throbbing
quietly because I paid it no attention
anymore—until it had permission to be felt. And
then, it made sure it was fully felt.

I was relatively disengaged of this particular
situation, had set boundaries of detachment, and
had done the work. Really I had.

Bessel Van Der Kolk, author of The Body Keeps
the Score, says, "Our bodies are the texts that
carry the memories and therefore remembering
is no less than reincarnation."

Despite best efforts to do the work, set
boundaries, keep myself safe and healed and all
the things, I have learned that layers run deep
and the more healing I do—the more broken I
see that I am.

It is ok to be broken. To be broken is also to be free.

Our bodies are powerful and beg for us to listen and honor these qualities. They are the secret keepers of memories that we have detached from, they are the security guards of emotions we can no longer feel, and they are the authors of meanings we assign to these memories and emotions that tell us stories about our worth and value.

Back to forgiving—it is funny. I knew that I needed to forgive myself, for not knowing what I didn't know, for not doing something sooner, blah blah, but I never looked at forgiveness as giving an offering to my own self, my own body, my own spirit —gifting it whatever it needs whenever it needs it. This is the meaning of of "giving completely" that I can make sense of right now. This sits well with my soul.

Granting permission to myself to release emotions from myself and also really feel them is a good big step. Labeling these emotions and unpacking them. Another step. Looking at patterns and examining energy and making intentions to shift into healthy realms, another step. It's beautiful work, the work of forgiveness. I now realize what it means when people say—it is for ourselves, not for others.

My giving in this way, with this intention, completes me. It makes me whole, human, beautiful, vulnerable and real. My struggle to give in this way also makes me whole, human, beautiful, vulnerable and real. I have found that the process of forgiveness is the whole point of the word and the reality of the concept. The process and the outcome are one. Like the perfect union of two souls meeting as one.

Forgiveness is for giving to ourselves what we had hoped someone would have given to us. I can give myself, my soul honor, love, loyalty, and cherish me through this process while recognizing that I am disappointed, hurt, sad those things were not given to me in _______ situation. We can give this gift to ourselves freely and completely. This gift does not depend on an apology from someone who will never give it, rectified behavior that you may never see, or a change of heart that will never come. It only depends on how much we can love ourselves by saying, "I deserve to give myself what I needed/wanted/desired in the circumstance and also, eff off to the hope that

this situation will ever be something different
that it is or was."

I like this reframing, because it takes the focus
off the hurt/harm/pain person _______ caused by
doing ________, and instead it places the focus
on gifting the ability to ourselves feel our
emotions, to love ourselves, and to shift our
energy from something destructive to something
productive, which is also a beautiful symbol of
forgiveness in every sense of the word. Doing
this also allows us to move on, move through,
and move past the situation that caused us
_______ instead of dwelling on it to send our
light-giving energy to places and people where it
is best honored, cherished, and held in the high
regard it should be.

When we have been hurt, we often become
numb to our own emotions. We can feel like
strangers in our own bodies. We have trouble
even feeling like we know who we are.

I believe in forgiveness even if it is for selfish
reasons.
Let me be selfish. Let me give myself the things
that were not given to me when I needed them
most. Let me feel what it is like to not be numb.
Let me be able to feel what it is like to feel my

own emotions again. Let me feel what it is like to not feel like a stranger in my own body. Let me feel what it is like to know me again.

Let me give me back to me.

That is the work of forgiveness.

The Principal

I received a call from the Principal at the middle school. Alarmed, I'm sure he could sense the edge in my voice, as he immediately reassured me that everything was ok. This was a good call. He wanted to share some information with me regarding my son, Krew.

Krew is in 7th grade. He sits with a group of friends at lunch, which is important to him because some of these friends are not in any of his classes. He really enjoys his social time with friends.

The Principal said that the at the end of the lunch period one particular day, the lunch trays were completely scattered and not stacked the right way one on top of each other. The trays were a big mess and thrown carelessly on top of the other trays and they weren't laying flat, but falling over.

The Principal said he came back into the lunch room a few minutes later while the students were leaving to go to class and noticed that the lunch trays were neatly stacked to lay flat, someone had taken time to organize them nicely and clean up the mess for the lunch ladies.

He looked around and noticed Krew sitting quietly and asked, "Krew did you do this? Did you fix the mess of lunch trays?"

Krew just smiled and replied, "Well, someone had to do it. Why not me?"

The Principal commented on how kind-hearted he found Krew to be and although this was not a huge deal, it is something that he doesn't see everyday and wanted me to know. I'm sure it wasn't the coolest thing to do: leave your friends during lunch to go clean up other people's mess of trays, but here my son is, doing it so the lunch ladies don't have to.

And you know what, I am glad the Principal took time to call and tell me this about my kid.

Because I realized, out of all the things I hope my child would be, most of all and most important is kind.

The Sexiness

For much of my life, I was taught that a woman's body covered and hidden and that women needed to do, act, and be a certain way in order to be acceptable in the eyes of others. I reject these ideas now. I love my body. I love my sexiness. I love my playful presency, my vibrant energy. I will never supress these things about me again, and instead, only continue to embrace who I was made to be and love who I have become.

But...

Truth be told, I *still* work everyday to undo this messaging I received much of my life about what women should be. Sexiness was a sin. Too much skin was immodest. Sensuality was not a good quality.

I spent a lot of my life trying to not be these things. Throwing out my red lipstick and instead wearing bare minimal makeup. Trading my four-inch heels for flats. Wearing longer dresses that were sure to cover my knees and for sure my thighs. Wearing camis under every top so it wouldn't be too low cut.

And for what? To be accepted in a culture that told me that a woman was someone who gave up her own identity for the emotional comfort of everyone else. And it wasn't about what women wore—it was about letting women have their own expression and opinions and respecting those just as much as anyone else. I realized that for me, that was not a healthy culture that honors the essence or individuality of women. And so me, my short skirts, high heels, opinions and ideas walked away from it.

In unpacking all of this, I had to actively grieve for the parts of myself that were muted and made invisible to make others more comfortable with my presence. This was hard and sad and I still catch myself sometimes with a cloud of grief for the me that never was.

But also lucky for me, I have the whole rest of my time here to explore who I am, how I want to express myself and the ways in which I desire to show up on my own stage of life. There are no imaginary man-made up rules in my theatre, only to embrace all parts of me—even the ones that once-upon-a-time were told needed to be kept hidden, sacrificed, and given up.

And those parts—you know, the ones I had to hide, cover, downplay to make others feel better—well, those parts are the ones that I am now giving to center stage.

The Care Package

The care package that taught me about exactly what I needed to know.

Most of this weekend, I was super tired, sleeping most of the days, had body aches and overall just feeling kind of run down. I was able to rest this weekend alone, but my kids are back with me today for a 10 day super packed stretch of soccer games, practices, gymnastics, tutoring, meetings and appointments.

I mentioned this to a good friend of mine—the feeling of overwhelm and exhaustion even just thinking about the week I've got ahead of me on top of feeling run down and under the weather.

The next thing I knew, I had the most thoughtful care package on my doorstep, complete with six pizzas for us for the week, tons of paper plates to last to avoid doing dishes, different medication of all types independently labeled, vapor rub, shakes, tea, chapstick and my personal favorite—eucalyptus oil for my bath. A kind note read: "Whatever I thought that Lesley needed to survive this week, that's what I put in here."

I have to be honest— I stared at the package for a few minutes trying to figure out how on earth another person could know me this well and be so incredibly thoughtful all at the same time, but also what on earth I did to deserve this profound compassion from someone else, who likely didn't even know how impactful it was to me at that moment.

I'm used to being strong and doing it alone. I rarely ask for help and typically just handle my shit. Accepting service in such a personal way is just not something I often do. I sat with this feeling for minute—what was it that I felt exactly? Then it occurred to me that this was the feeling of being *known*—how powerful and special that is, particularly to someone who has always been independent and strong and has rarely let others know her in a personal way.

Feeling "known" can feel scary for those of us who have experienced alot in life. It can feel like band-aids ripped off for our wounds to be on display. It's like my subconscious instantly feels exposed by its vulnerabilities and that means weakness and that means something to hurt me with. Which of course, means trust is the only antidote.

And yeah, this was just a care package, but it was like a dose of therapy for me today. Seeing just how letting my own trust develop with special people who want to know me and show me they know me can actually be healing in more ways than one.

The Red Flags

I've been unpacking some heavy things lately. As I open myself into desiring deeper relationships, taking brave steps forward to actually allow myself to yearn for a partner to share life with, and admit—yes this is what I want eventually in life—I also feel obligated to do some tough love work on my own tendencies in relationships to show up in ways that will allow me to avoid pain, minimize betrayal, and somehow be free from heartache.

In learning about myself and examining my own patterns crafted to so carefully and cautiously avoid getting hurt, I can undoubtedly say that these patterns within us that aim to protect our fragile hearts do no such thing.

Instead, the patterns help us, remind us, and prompt us to slow down, be careful, be cautious, ask a million questions, be curious, take time when needed, take note of red flags, and cultivate cultivate cultivate and listen listen listen to our own intuition. Be thankful for them. Your patterns will weed out anyone who cannot or will not do the work. And HINT: You want someone who will do the work for you, for them, and the relationship.

For trauma survivors, those who have experienced emotional inconsistency within a "loving" relationship, anyone who has experience with intimate betrayal, or has felt the sting of emotional anorexia being used as a tool against them by a partner who is supposed to be caring, loving, supportive, kind, generous, gentle, and tender-hearted—we can easily get confused by where the line is between how our trauma is manifesting in our relationships and what our intuition is trying to tell us (in some cases scream to us.)

This is difficult work. And at the risk of sounding completely cliche—literally all the signs you've heard before are the ones you need to pay attention to. And chances are, your trauma IS being activated because your intuition wants to be heard this time, loud and clear. Off the top of my head, here are the signs I don't want to ignore as I continue to brave this journey of finding love after grief:

1. Someone who pressures you into rushing a relationship/commitment before you are ready. Like they want to talk about committing after a

week—this is because their ego is fragile and they cannot handle the fact that you are allowed to make up your mind on your own without pressure to commit.

2. Someone who uses manipulative communication—this includes passive aggressiveness—as a way to get what they want regularly and makes no effort to change this.

3. Inconsistency between their words and actions. This looks like hot and cold behaviors. They say all the right things, but their actions don't align.

4. Emotional inconsistency—one day they are SO attentive, the next they pullback. You feel like you are on some crazy-train-roller-coaster, but if you bring it up, then it's your fault. Yay!

5. Then when you ask them about the inconsistencies, they gaslight you, saying it's all in your head, work was busy, blame your for asking about it, call you paranoid or make you feel guilty like it is your problem. (It's not.)

6. Not to mention they are FULL of excuses. Like endless endless excuses. Voicemails full of excuses of why they didn't call/text/ make plans/

blew you off/ etc. Helpful tip: Many of these excuses will be disguised as actually being considerate. Like they didn't stay when they knew that was the most important thing to you, because they didn't want
to keep you up with an imaginary cough they started coming down with that day.

7. Be careful not to mistake excuses for explanations. An explanation will include owning a misunderstanding, an apology if needed, clarifying information about a certain situation—excuses are full of not-so-legitimate reasons they couldn't or didn't do something that was important to you.

8. HINT: there is usually no legitimate reason for this ^^^. If they wanted to, they would. Think about all those times they love-bombed you, paying attention to little details, sending verbose texts about how much you were their world, taking you on meaningful dates, making an effort to show up for you in the way you needed—-they are capable, you've seen it, so if they aren't doing this—they don't want to. This IS the crux of pulling the rug of love and emotional connection out from under you. It is awful and it is highly confusing. And again, it's

not your fault or anything you did. No matter how much they try to make you feel like it was.

9. Love-bombing—sounds like, "goodnight gorgeous, you are everything I've ever wanted blah blah bullshit"—this also includes future faking promises—making you fall in love with the dream of the future with them. It is fake. Trust me, real love takes time and doesn't have to try so damn hard to cover for inadequacies that it has deep insecurities about.

10. Using what they know about you to hurt you. Do they know your deepest fear of being abandoned or feeling rejected? Just wait and give them a bit of time to make sure they fully craft some situation where they can make this deepest fear come true just for you. That is how much they love you! Don't you feel lucky yet?

11. They usually show you early on who they are and what they're all about. Don't give second chances. Cut it off early. And don't go back.

12. Pay attention to how your health is in the relationship and what your body tells you. Are your headaches increasing? Feeling anxious? Stressed? This is your intuition tell you stay

away and your trauma getting triggered because this person is not for you.

13. Please please please don't mistake chaos for chemistry. You are used to chaos as a form of what you think is love. This can be a very powerful feeling. A deep physical attraction. It can feel like amazing chemistry. It's not. Butterflies are not always good—it is your body on high alert—your senses going off like alarm bells.

14. They make you feel ashamed for your trauma, your needs, or your wants. They leave the emotional labor for you to do, sure, they'll "agree" to do all sorts of things that sound great and connective, but when it comes down to it, they never actually will take the initiative to do this—you will feel like you are carrying this load. Alone. Because you are. Sounds fun right!?

15. They cut you down in ways that seem harmless but aren't. This includes "jokes" about you, telling you that are aren't attractive when you ____, insulting or degrading you in ways that sound like a compliment (for an older woman, your body is great). Just don't even with

someone who does any of this. They will show this to you very very early—listen and leave.

16. As much as hope seems all but lost for these souls—You can depend on them for one very consistent thing: They will always always always make sure to kick you when you are down. Like at the worst possible time, they will deliver the gut punches to you. Have no doubt in this. You can depend on them!

17. You feel like an open book—they know your friends, your schedule, you've let them in to your life, but it is not mutual—you've never been even invited to their place (HUGE RED FLAG, indicates major deception), never met their friends (do they even have any), and feel sucked dry and stripped bare after they discard you, like who was that person even? Did you really know them? No—most likely you had no idea who they even were deep down.

18. They try to convince you that the connection is solid when you know deep down that it isn't. Something felt off and you listened to them instead of listening to you. It's ok, this happens because 1. They are manipulators 2. You want so much to be loved and to trust. Don't put your list of non-negotiables a aside just because they try

to convince you that it's not important. If you want someone with intellect, make sure you don't settle for someone who says they don't ever read. If you want someone who shares your values, don't settle for someone whose values involve making fun of those people who are different. If you want someone who is healthy mentally, make sure you choose someone who doesn't let their ego run the show or their emotions. You are an amazing person with depth and heart, don't settle for someone who has neither.

19. Do they always ditch you on a Saturday night? Do you never hardly see them on the prime weekend times? Hate to break it to you, but you can call yourself Thursday girl and know that there is another who is Friday girl and Saturday is likely reserved for a regular side piece. Ewe. No thanks.

20. They say ALL the right things to make you feel ok to pursue the relationship….no they hardly ever do drugs or smoke or whatever it is…then down the road you get to know them and find out, yeah actually they light up practically daily and no they don't care if you wouldn't have gone out with them if you knew this in the first place. Oh and also no, they aren't

giving it up for you either. Because you are meaningless. They choose a high over you....that's quality right there!

Perhaps one final little tip I'd leave here is the tendency we as empathetic survivors have is to put our own needs aside in order to acquiesce to people who just don't give two f%#€s about us. This is because we have developed the need to not treat others like we were once treated, we can have real trouble believing awful exists as it does, even though we have seen it before. This is especially true when we feel somewhat healed and brave enough to share parts of ourselves with others. Surely they won't hurt us with it, only to find out that we gaslight ourselves about this too.

I will also say that there is nothing more important than having safe, secure, stable people around you and in your life, that can just be with you with no expectations in return, respect your boundaries, keep your trust, hold space for the work you are doing, hold your trauma in their open palms like it is the most fragile little butterfly with broken wings, encouraging it to just exist there, knowing that those wings will eventually heal themselves, mended with threads of patience, time, and unconditional acceptance.

These people—do not let them go. And remind yourself, you deserve someone who can be oh-so-gentle with those broken butterfly wings because one day those wings will be repaired into beautiful colors and patterns that will let you fly.

The Green Flags

Today, I intended to make a list of Green Flags because my OCD felt bad that I made a list of Red Flags without having a Green Flag list too. So I started thinking of a list of healthy, good signs in someone, and I realized that there really, really are great, great good, good men around me. And all I needed to do was to share some of the ways in which they have shown up for me. And how they keep showing up. These are all Green Flags I have experienced in the last few weeks. And that is also a Green Flag.

Green flags look like:

Men who will pick up and answer anytime I call. They will always lend a listening ear and me a priority. And I call them because they make me want to call them.

Men who will apologize for other men's actions.

Men who compliment me meaningfully, without expecting anything in return but because it makes me smile and I can tell they truly mean it.

Men who drop off a care package, complete with eucalyptus oil for my bath, when I'm sick just because they know it will make me feel seen and heard and known.

Men who are patient. Oh gosh they are patient. And kind. And gentle. And tender. And loving. And damn. All the things. But most of all—they are comfortable in this being. Because this is SO sexy and safe.

Men who make a consistent effort to get to know me, like I am worth everything and more in their eyes.

Men who actually want to talk about substantive things. For hours.

Men who question everything in life as much as I do.

Men who read and learn and who introduce me to new ideas and feed my brain because they know this feeds my soul.

Men who will wait and not rush for the chemistry to be right and when it is, it really is.

Men who forgive me when I am impatient with
them for no reason other than another man
treated me badly that day.

Men who have open conversations about life,
love, experiences, expectations with me because
they get that this is how to do it.

Men drop off pizza for my kids that they've
never met because they understand how dinner
is sometimes the last thought on my mind as a
single mom.

Men who like who I am, what I stand for, read
what I write, want me to write more, and think
I'm a badass because they know and care about
my journey.

Men who literally know every little last
vulnerability I have at this very moment. And I
know that I can trust them with that, completely.

Men who I don't have to hide the parts of myself
that aren't all the pretty from.

Men who see me with no makeup, tear-stained
face, wearing old sweats and my hair in some
hot mess of a weird bun that has been in since

yesterday, and still make me feel like the most beautiful woman in the world.

Men who go out of their way to not hurt me in the ways they know I am most sensitive to.

Men who build me up in those fears and make me feel like I can conquer anything with them behind me.

Men who are 100% comfortable in their own sexuality to talk about all the things because they know this what builds chemistry.

Men who respect a boundary when I set it. They don't take my boundary as a personal affront to their ego. They treat me like a person who can make up her own mind and give me the space to do so.

Men who are consistent in action and words. They are reliable. If they say they will be here/do something, they show up/they do it.

Men who know what it means to truly repair. They can own their stuff and apologize if needed without assigning blame to me. And we grow can together.

Men who don't blame women for their problems. instead they are thoughtful, respectful, and non-judgmental particularly when they talk about their former relationships.

Men who really don't send the same exact messages to dozens of different women. Men who want me. Not just any woman. Me. Because I am me.

Men who don't center themselves in everything and understand that it is not an issue of how I fit into their idea of what *they* want, but instead how we both can fulfill needs in each other mutually.

Men who understand that my anxiousness, wants, and needs within a relationship is a chance to connect and build trust with me and never something to judge me or put me down for.

Men who continually show me new parts of my own worth, instead of me feeling like I have to prove it to them.

I hope to keep adding to this list of Green Flags, as I continue to navigate through the journey of unpacking my own stuff and being open to what the universe has in store for me.

When we find these people, the ones who are mature, emotionally open, and trustworthy, it can sometimes trigger us to question why they exist in this way or what they are going to want from us in return or when they are going to take off their mask and show us their true self—because we know the mask falls off always and we are so used to "niceness" being used in a manipulative way and for anything but just existing as part of a healthy relationship. Some of us also do not identify or equate green flags as anything having to do with love and even positive, good qualities in the first place because of our past experiences. We simply do not understand and cannot make sense of green flags. But we can learn!

This is all the work that we must do of reframing our own ideas and definitions of what we really want, we truly we need, and what we know is most important for us to have in our relationships. And as much as it may sound daunting, we want, we need someone who will learn to respect our walls, scale them if needed, scrub them with a toothbrush if they are showing

signs of wear, but also help us install windows
and maybe eventually screendoors.

And the healthy men will show up with their
toolkits ready.

The Full Circle

92

Never ever did I think I would get to a point where I would say these words out loud: I wouldn't change anything about my life—not the grief, pain, trauma, or loss—because ultimately it has made me who I am and made my life what it is: full of resilience that I never knew, strength I have come to count on, and a knowledge that I can get through hard things.

As of woman of 40, my life looks so different than I could have ever imagined it would. I'm a divorced, single, working mom, who has experienced her share of loss and grief, pain and trauma. And there is absolutely nothing I would change about it.

Because, it also means that I have experienced the healing power of self-care, embraced my authenticity, and reclaimed my inner authority. Stepping into this milestone has been an amazing life event, where I can truly say I am happy with who I am, what I stand for, and the life I lead. I am so incredibly happy to have beautiful photos that reflect on the outside all of

the beautiful work, determination, and resilience
that I possess on the inside.

We so often admire a woman's ability to have
strength, courage, tenacity, resilience, but we do
not see what is underneath all of that---what it
took for her to truly find herself and cultivate
those qualities. This type of inner work can be
challenging, reflective, emotional, and
multi-layered. It is messy and chaotic.
But in the end, a beautiful picture comes
together of a woman who embraces the beauty
of a perfectly imperfect path.

I am my fears, my failures, my successes, my
shortcomings. Those things all make me who I
am and that is beautiful because it is me. I don't
need to be perfect to be worthwhile.

Loving myself is only dependent on me, not
anyone else, and that is a cathartic, empowering
thought.